# Miguel Tanco
# Count on me

At home everyone
has their own passion.
My dad has one.

And my mum
has another one.

My brother loves music
and he's getting very good at it.

At school there are all sorts of activities
that could be my passion.

I've tried them all,
but they just aren't for me.

There is one thing I really like, though . . .

# MATHS!

Maths is all around us.
It's often hidden
and I love finding it.

There are geometric patterns
in the playground.

And when we go to the lake
I skip stones to see the concentric
circles form in the water.

We live in a world of shapes
and I like to play with them.

It's fun for me to find
the perfect curve . . .

And solve difficult group problems.

I use maths every day.

I know that my passion
can be hard to understand.

But there are infinite ways to see the world . . .

And maths is one of them.

# FRACTALS

A fractal is a never-ending pattern.
The patterns used in fractals can be different ~~sizes~~
sizes and directions and are used over and over
to create an ongoing construction. I see lots of
fractals in nature!

fractal of three

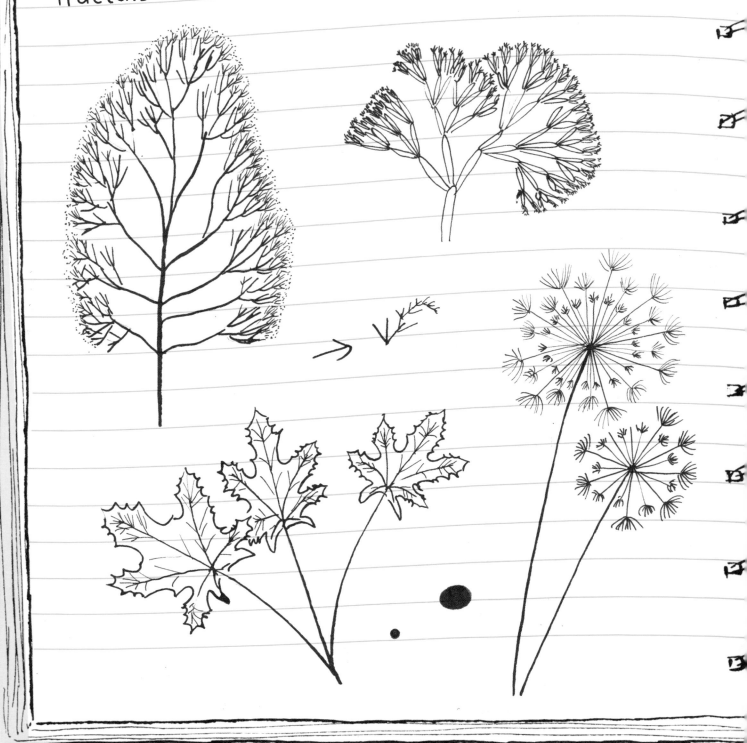

# BASIC POLYGONS →  □

A <u>polygon</u> is a shape with straight sides and is fully closed. Polygons can have any number of sides. I love to find polygons hidden in objects.

45°

milk

# CONCENTRIC CIRCLES ⟶

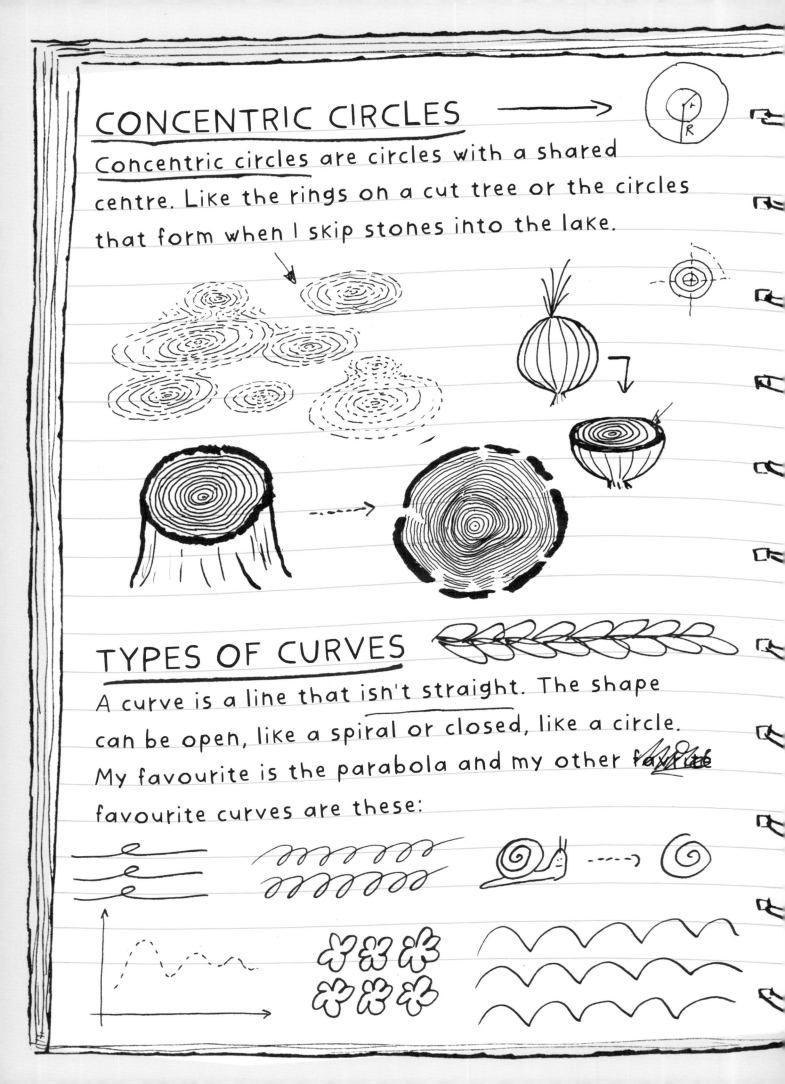

Concentric circles are circles with a shared centre. Like the rings on a cut tree or the circles that form when I skip stones into the lake.

# TYPES OF CURVES

A curve is a line that isn't straight. The shape can be open, like a spiral or closed, like a circle. My favourite is the parabola and my other favourite curves are these:

# SOLID FIGURES ⟶

Solid figures are shapes that are three-dimensional. I know the names of some solid figure shapes:

Sphere

Cylinder

Rectangular Prism

Pyramid

Cube

Cone

# TYPES OF TRAJECTORIES

A trajectory is a curved path on which an object moves through space. I see trajectories when a football is kicked or someone is on a swing. I like to try to predict the trajectories of my paper aeroplanes.

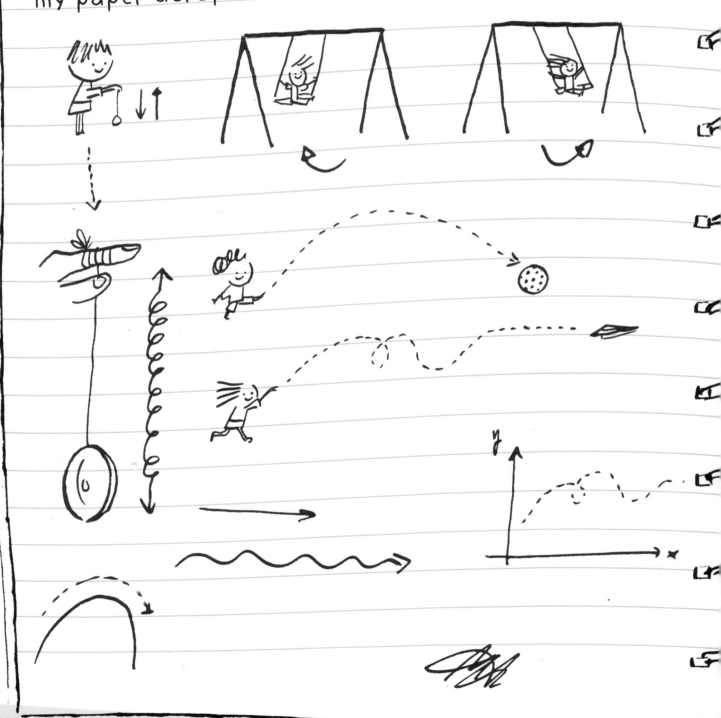

# KINDS OF SETS

A <u>set</u> is a group or a collection of things that have at least one common ~~class~~ characteristic. They can be intersected, added or divided into smaller sets, called <u>sub-sets</u>.

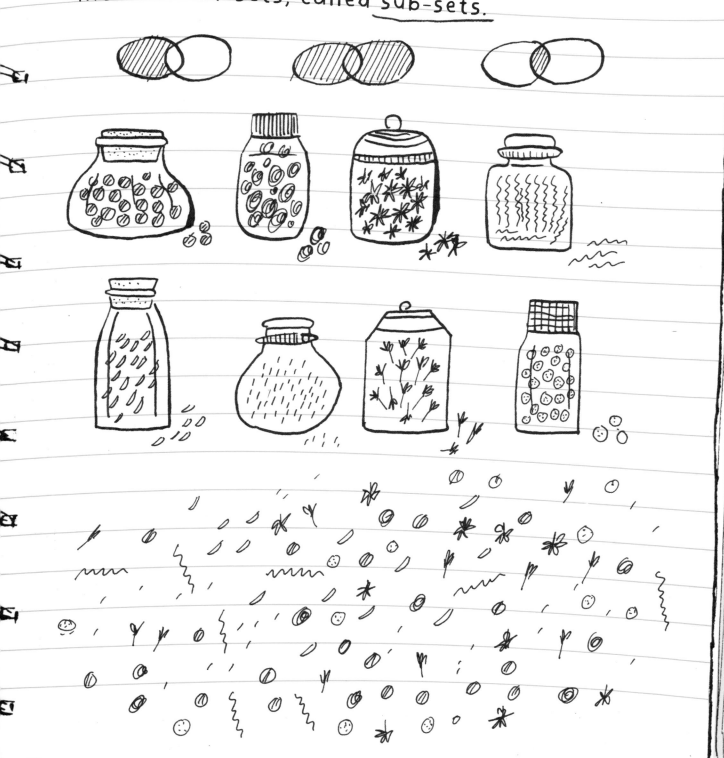

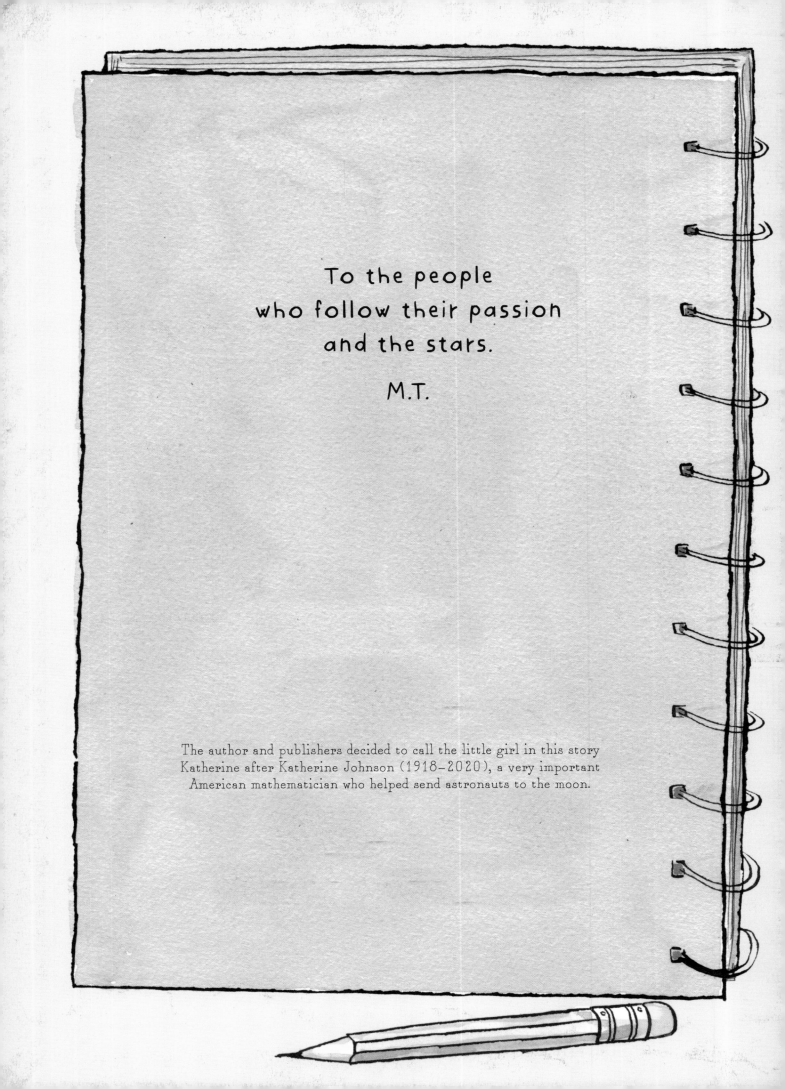

To the people
who follow their passion
and the stars.

M.T.

The author and publishers decided to call the little girl in this story Katherine after Katherine Johnson (1918–2020), a very important American mathematician who helped send astronauts to the moon.